PIRANHAS

BY MARY BERENDES

The Child's World

Published by The Child's World®
1980 Lookout Drive • Mankato, MN 56003-1705
800-599-READ • www.childsworld.com

ACKNOWLEDGMENTS
The Child's World®: Mary Berendes, Publishing Director
Olivia Gregory: Editing
Pamela J. Mitsakos: Photo Research

PHOTO CREDITS
© Andreiadis/Dreamstime.com: 8; Andrey Armyagov/Shutterstock.com: 5;
col/Shutterstock.com: 17; DanBrandenburg/iStock.com: 7; georgeclerk/
iStock.com: 15; Hayati Kayhan/Shutterstock.com: cover, 1; ilbusca/iStock.
com: 7; l i g h t p o e t/Shutterstock.com: 21; nicolasdecorte/Shutterstock.
com: 19; Oleg Golovnev/BigStock.com: 12; PhotoDisc: 23, 24; Santi
Rodriguez/Shutterstock.com: 11

ISBN 9781631437502
LCCN 2014945412

Printed in the United States of America
Mankato, MN
November, 2014
PA02242

ABOUT THE AUTHOR

Mary Berendes has loved books and writing for as long as she can remember. An author of over 40 children's books, Mary especially enjoys writing about nature and animals. Mary has long been a collector of antique books and owns several that are more than 200 years old. She lives in Minnesota.

TABLE OF CONTENTS

4 Meet the Piranha!

6 Trap-Like Teeth

9 Tropical Fish

10 Different Kinds

13 Tiny Babies

14 Anything Eaters

16 Feeding Frenzy!

18 Piranha Enemies

20 Important Fish

22 *Glossary*

23 *To Find Out More*

24 *Index*

On the cover: These red-bellied piranhas are swimming in a tank.

MEET THE PIRANHA!

"Piranha" means "toothed fish."

"Piranha" can be pronounced either puh-RAH-nuh or puh-RAHN-yah.

A river flows slowly through the South American jungle. Under the water's surface, animals of all kinds swim and live. Near the shore, colorful fish are splashing and jumping in a large group. They are biting away pieces of meat from a dead catfish. What could these hungry fish be? They're piranhas!

Red-bellied piranhas seem to sparkle when the sunlight hits their sides.

TRAP-LIKE TEETH

It's hard to tell the difference between male and female piranhas just by looking at them.

Piranhas keep replacing their teeth throughout their lives, so their teeth are always very sharp.

Piranhas are beautiful fish. Many are brightly colored with red, green, or black markings. They have round, flat bodies and stubby snouts. But piranhas are best known for their teeth. The teeth are triangular, strong, and razor sharp. The piranha's lower jaw sticks out farther than its upper jaw. The teeth close together like a trap. Once a piranha bites something, it can tear at it easily.

A fisherman caught this red-bellied piranha. You can see how sharp the teeth are!

TROPICAL FISH

Piranhas are freshwater **tropical** fish. They come from rivers, lakes, and streams in several parts of South America. They live in places where the water is warm all year long. Some of the most famous rivers with piranhas are the Amazon, the Orinoco, and the La Plata.

Sometimes piranhas appear in other parts of the world where they don't belong. They have been found in North America and even as far away as the Ukraine. They got to these places because people kept them as pets and then turned them loose. If conditions are right, **invasive** animals such as these can live and grow, causing damage to other plants and animals.

Piranhas don't live in South America's mountain lakes or streams. The water is too cold.

Piranhas usually rest at night and are most active at dawn.

Red-bellied piranhas are most often found in the Amazon River.

DIFFERENT KINDS

Some scientists think piranhas swim in groups to protect themselves from enemies.

Some piranhas can grow to nearly 24 inches (61 cm) long.

There are about 25 different kinds, or **species**, of piranhas. The most common is the red-bellied piranha. Its name comes from the bright red color on its underside. Red-bellied piranhas can grow up to 16 inches (41 cm) long. They often have gold or silver backs with darker tails.

Another type of piranha is the black piranha. It has red eyes and very strong jaws. An adult black piranha's jaws are so strong, it can bite through a piece of wood!

Male red-bellied piranhas have brighter bellies than females.

TINY BABIES

Little is known about how piranhas have their young. Most scientists agree that piranhas mate during the rainy season, when the water is deeper. They also think that adult females lay eggs on floating water plants or in nests made in the mud.

When the eggs hatch, tiny piranhas swim out and hide in nearby plants and rocks. When they are big enough, the young piranhas swim out in the open and join the adults.

When piranhas build nests, they clear an area by moving stones and chewing up plants.

Both piranha parents guard their eggs.

A piranha defending its eggs might be more likely to bite or attack.

This baby redeye piranha is hiding in some rocks. Redeye piranhas grow to be about 16 inches (41 cm) long.

ANYTHING EATERS

Piranhas rarely attack healthy **prey**. Instead, they prefer to eat dead or dying animals.

Piranha babies might eat each other if they are hungry and there is little other food.

Piranhas eat almost anything. Some eat seeds or fruits that fall into the water. Others wait for insects or smaller fish to swim by. Some piranhas eat the tails and fins of larger fish. A few kinds even bite the toes of animals that walk or swim through the water. Most piranhas are also **scavengers** that eat dead animals. By eating dead creatures, piranhas keep rivers and lakes clean.

Red-bellied piranhas usually eat insects, worms, and other fish.

FEEDING FRENZY!

Piranhas can tell when there's a single drop of blood in 50 gallons (189 l) of water.

An animal splashing and making noise in the water can cause a piranha feeding frenzy.

Piranhas' taste buds cover their bodies. That helps the fish decide whether things floating or swimming by would be good to eat.

Piranhas might go for days without food and then stuff themselves when they get the chance.

Piranhas like blood. In fact, they can even smell it! When an animal is bleeding in the water, a few piranhas will swim toward it. If they can, they bite little pieces from the animal. That makes the animal bleed some more. As more piranhas smell the blood, they swim toward the animal. Soon the water is full of hungry, biting piranhas. This is called a **feeding frenzy**.

When piranhas eat, they use their teeth only to cut and bite. They never chew their food. Instead, they swallow it whole. That way, they can eat very quickly. With so many piranhas eating during a feeding frenzy, the food disappears fast. Each piranha eats quickly to get all the food it can!

Piranhas usually leave people and larger animals alone. But during certain times of the year, they attack more often. When the weather is very dry, the piranhas' rivers and lakes begin to dry up. When this happens, the piranhas have less room and less food. They begin to attack everything in the water—even each other! During the dry season, injured or weak animals can be eaten quickly if they enter waters where hungry piranhas live.

The most dangerous piranhas, though, are the ones in a feeding frenzy. They are very excited and will snap and bite at almost anything. If you put your hand in the water during a feeding frenzy, the piranhas would probably bite you by mistake. That's why South Americans stay out of the water when piranhas are in a feeding frenzy. Otherwise, they would be food for the piranhas, too!

People in South America often swim in water where there are piranhas, but they are careful. It's not a good idea to go swimming near piranhas if you have an open cut!

These red-bellied piranhas live in a tank. They are all swimming toward the same prey at feeding time.

PIRANHA ENEMIES

If a piranha gets caught on a hook and line, other piranhas might attack it.

People who fish for piranhas must handle them carefully when they take them out of the water. Otherwise, they might get bitten.

Even though piranhas can be dangerous, many other animals like to eat them. Wading birds and fish eat young and small piranhas. Larger piranhas are often eaten by crocodiles called caimans. Many people like to eat piranhas, too. South Americans use everything from strings to nets to catch these delicious fish.

This caiman in Brazil has caught a piranha to eat.

IMPORTANT FISH

Piranha attacks on people are very rare. In fact, there are no solid reports of any person being killed by piranhas.

Piranhas can live to be about eight years old.

People in South America use piranha teeth as cutting tools.

Piranhas are very important. They keep rivers and lakes clean by eating dead fish and other animals. Fruit-eating piranhas help, too. By carrying fruit seeds in their waste, they spread different kinds of plants throughout the rivers and lakes.

Scary movies and stories show piranhas as mean, angry fish that like to attack people and animals. But that isn't really true. They might be dangerous, but they don't bite to be mean. They bite when they are hungry, scared, or excited.

Although some people keep piranhas as pets, some countries do not allow that. Their governments do not want people turning piranhas loose in local waters. But many zoos and aquariums have piranhas for people to watch and study.

Maybe one day you'll actually travel to South America. If you do, keep an eye out for the colorful piranha! Instead of being afraid, you can see piranhas for the beautiful and important creatures they really are.

These baby red-bellied piranhas will hopefully grow up into adults.

GLOSSARY

feeding frenzy (FEE-ding FREN-zee) When animals are in a feeding frenzy, they eat quickly—in a wild and excited way. Piranhas sometimes go into feeding frenzies.

invasive (in-VAY-siv) Invasive species are ones people bring to lands where they don't belong and where they can do harm. Releasing pet fish such as piranhas can turn them into invasive species.

prey (PRAY) Prey are animals that other animals hunt as food. Piranhas don't usually attack healthy prey.

scavengers (SKAV-un-jerz) Animals that are scavengers will feed on whatever garbage they find, including dead animals. Piranhas are scavengers.

species (SPEE-sheez) An animal species is a group of animals that share the same features and can have babies only with animals in the same group. There are about 25 species of piranha.

tropical (TRAH-pih-kull) Tropical areas are those that have warm, moist weather all year long. Piranhas are tropical fish.

TO FIND OUT MORE

Read It!

Ganeri, Anita. *Piranha*. Chicago, IL: Heinemann Library, 2011.

Gish, Melissa. *Piranhas*. Mankato, MN: Creative Education, 2012.

Jackson, Tom. *Piranhas and Other Small Deadly Creatures*. New York: Crabtree, 2009.

Storad, Conrad J. *Piranhas.* Minneapolis, MN: Lerner Publications, 2009.

On the Web

Visit our home page for lots of links about piranhas:
www.childsworld.com/links

Note to Parents, Teachers, and Librarians: We routinely check our Web links to make sure they're safe, active sites—so encourage your readers to check them out!

INDEX

Appearance, 6, 10

Babies, 13, 14, 20
black piranha, 10

Caiman, 18

Eggs, 13
enemies, 18

Feeding frenzy, 16, 17

Importance of, 14, 20

Jaws, 6, 10

Location, 4, 9

Nests, 13

as **P**ets, 9, 20
prey, 14, 16, 17
pronunciation, 4

Red-bellied piranha, 3, 4, 6, 9, 10, 14, 17, 20
redeye piranha, 13

Scavengers, 14
species, 10

Teeth, 6, 16, 20